JBIOG
Ryan

Nolan Ryan

NOLAN RYAN

Hall of Fame
Baseball Superstar

William W.
Lace

Speeding Star

Speeding Star, an imprint of Enslow Publishers, Inc.

Library of Congress Cataloging-in-Publication Data

Lace, William W.
  Nolan Ryan : hall of fame baseball superstar / William W. Lace.
    pages cm. — (Hall of fame sports greats)
    Rev. ed. of Sports great Nolan Ryan
    Includes bibliographical references and index.
    Summary: "Read about Nolan Ryan, or "The Ryan Express," in this sports biography about the
  legendary pitcher who played 27 seasons in the Major Leagues. Follow his journey from living in a small
  town in Texas to becoming a Hall of Fame pitcher and Owner of the Texas Rangers"—Provided by
  publisher.
    ISBN 978-1-62285-025-9
    1. Ryan, Nolan, 1947-—Juvenile literature. 2. Baseball players—United States—Biography—uvenile
  literature. I. Title.
    GV865.R9L32 2013
    796.357092—dc23
    [B]
                        2013002669

Paperback ISBN: 978-1-62285-026-6   EPUB ISBN: 978-1-62285-028-0
Single-User PDF ISBN: 978-1-62285-029-7   Multi-User PDF ISBN: 978-1-62285-148-5

Printed in the United States of America
052013 Lake Book Manufacturing, Inc., Melrose Park, IL
10 9 8 7 6 5 4 3 2 1

To Our Readers: We have done our best to make sure all Internet addresses in this book were active and
appropriate when we went to press. However, the author and the Publisher have no control over, and assume
no liability for, the material available on those Internet sites or on other Web sites they may link to. Any com-
ments or suggestions can be sent by e-mail to comments@speedingstar.com or to the address below:

Speeding Star
Box 398, 40 Industrial Road
Berkeley Heights, NJ 07922
USA
www.speedingstar.com

Photo Credits: AP Images, pp. 13, 17, 23, 26, 38; AP Images/Bill Janscha, p. 7; AP Images/Chris O'Meara,
p. 57; AP Images/David Jennings, p. 60; AP Images/F. Carter Smith, p. 46; AP Images/Frank Franklin II, p.
28; AP Images/Houston Chronicle, p. 11; AP Images/IK, p. 53; AP Images/Jeff Robbins, p. 34; AP Images/
Jerry W. Hoefer, p. 8; AP Images/Kevork Djansezian, pp. 1, 4; AP Images/Linda Kaye, p. 58; AP Images/
Paul Shane, p. 30; AP Images/PRNewsFoto/Nolan Ryan Beef, p. 55; AP Images/Ray Stubblebine, p. 42; AP
Images/Ron Heflin, p. 50; AP Images/Tim Johnson, p. 45; AP Images/Wally Fong, p. 21.

Cover Photo: AP Images/Kevork Djansezian

This book was originally published as *Sports Great Nolan Ryan* in 1993.

CONTENTS

Nolan Ryan rears back to throw one of his blazing fastballs.

Seventh Heaven

The night had grown late. It was nearly 10:30 p.m. But few of the 33,439 baseball fans in Arlington Stadium had left when the bottom of the ninth inning began. The Texas Rangers led Toronto, 3-0. The visiting Blue Jays didn't even have one hit. That fact was what kept the fans in their seats. Could the Rangers' Nolan Ryan pitch another no-hit game?

Ryan didn't dream that this game on May 1, 1991, would be anything special. Warming up he complained about sore muscles. Then a scar on the middle finger of his pitching hand began to bleed. "A no-hitter was the furthest thing from my mind," he said later.

Yet only two Blue Jays, Kelley Gruber and Joe Carter, had

managed to reach base, both on walks. The other 24 men to face Ryan had been retired, 15 of them on strikeouts! Now a no-hitter was on everyone's mind.

Ryan's first pitch to Manny Lee was a fastball low for ball one. Then he zipped another fastball. Lee swung, hitting a ground ball. Texas second baseman Julio Franco scooped it up and threw to first baseman Rafael Palmeiro: one out!

That brought up Devon White. He took a fastball high for ball one, then fouled off another to even the count. A called strike, another foul ball, and two balls made the count 3-2. Ryan went with his fastball again, and White hit another grounder to Franco. Again the second baseman cleanly fielded the ball and threw to Palmeiro: two out!

Next at bat was Roberto Alomar. Ryan had known Alomar since the Toronto second baseman was three years old. Ryan and Alomar's father, Sandy, had been teammates on the California Angels. In fact, Ryan had spent many hours teaching the six year old how to pitch. But now Roberto, at twenty-three, was standing between Ryan and a no-hitter.

The crowd kept up a steady roar. Everyone was standing, including Nolan's wife, Ruth. She had been sitting, her knees shaking, during the first two outs.

Alomar missed Ryan's first pitch and fouled off the second. Just one more strike was needed. But a fastball missed low for ball one, and after another foul, a curve was outside for ball two. Ryan got his signal from catcher Mike Stanley, wound up, and fired another fastball. It was his 122nd pitch of the night and

After throwing his seventh career no-hitter, Ryan is carried off the field by his Texas Rangers teammates.

registered 93 miles per hour on the radar gun. Alomar swung, but too late. Strike three, and the no-hitter was official!

Ryan flashed a broad smile. He strode off the mound and shook Stanley's hand before being surrounded by his shouting, leaping teammates. He had done it again! At forty-four, long past the age when most baseball players end their careers, Nolan Ryan had pitched his seventh no-hit game. No one had ever done that before. But, of course, when Ryan had pitched his fifth and sixth no-hitters, no one had ever done that either.

Later, in the middle of the locker-room celebration, Ryan was excited. He wasn't thinking about himself. Instead, he considered the people who had watched him. "It came here, in front of these fans on Arlington Appreciation Night, and they've been so supportive of me and my family since we came here a couple of years ago," he said.

The fans in Arlington had many reasons to support Ryan. In 1989, his first season with the Rangers, he had become the first pitcher ever to strike out 5,000 batters. In 1990 he pitched his sixth no-hitter and became only the 20th pitcher to win 300 games.

This seventh no-hitter, though, was special for Ryan. "This is my best," he said. "This is my most overpowering night."

Yet, the night was far from over. All the reporters wanted to

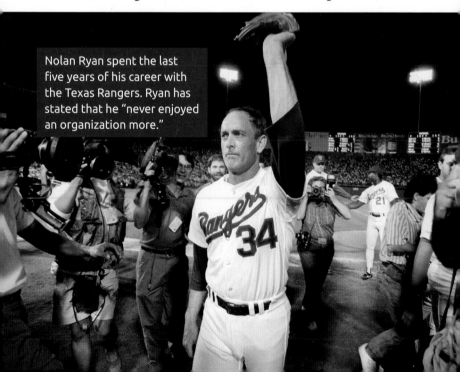

Nolan Ryan spent the last five years of his career with the Texas Rangers. Ryan has stated that he "never enjoyed an organization more."

talk to Ryan. Finally, he was able to take Ruth and some friends to a late dinner. By the time he got to bed it was 2:30 a.m.

Most people would have slept late the next morning, but not Nolan Ryan. At 9 a.m., he was the first player in the Rangers clubhouse, starting two hours of heavy weightlifting. No more time for celebration, only for the hard work of keeping an older man's body fit enough for a young man's game. Working out was not something Ryan especially liked, but it was something he had to do.

"You wake up in the morning when you're tired, and you have to come over here," he said. "It gets old, because it dominates so much of your time. But I know if I want to keep going, it's what I have to do."

In many ways, Ryan had come a long way from his hometown of Alvin, Texas. He had pitched in big cities and signed big-money contracts. But in other ways he had never left Alvin. Behind all the money and glamour, he remained a quiet, almost shy man. Ryan remained true to the values of honesty, hard work, loyalty, and respect for others that he had learned growing up.

Childhood Dreams

His family called Lynn Nolan Ryan, Jr., "Nolan." His father, Lynn Nolan Ryan, Sr., was called "Lynn." Nolan was born January 31, 1947, in Refugio, Texas. Six months later, his father was transferred by the oil company he worked for. The family moved to Alvin, a town twenty miles south of Houston. At the time, about 5,000 people lived there.

There wasn't much to Alvin then, and it's still not a big place. In spite of the enormous growth around Houston, Alvin's population has increased to only about 25,000 over the last sixty years.

There wasn't much for a kid to do besides school and sports. But young Nolan also had work to do. He was the youngest of six children. And when the oldest of Nolan's four sisters went to college, Nolan's father took a second job as a distributor for *The Houston Post*. So when Nolan was in second grade, he began working with his father. He and his older brother, Robert, would get up at 1 a.m. and help their father roll up and tie the 1,500 newspapers to be delivered. It would be 4 or 5 a.m. before they would get back to sleep until they woke up again for school.

When Ryan was old enough to drive, he helped deliver the papers. Later, the story was that Ryan gained his arm strength by throwing the newspapers. This made for a good story, but it wasn't true. Ryan pitched right-handed, but threw the papers left-handed, keeping his right hand on the steering wheel.

Nature and the outdoors were important to Ryan, as they were to most young boys in rural Texas. He loved hunting, and his most constant companion was Suzy, a white fox terrier.

The city of Houston received a major-league franchise in 1962, called the Houston Colt .45s. This is a picture of the opening day crowd for the franchise's first game.

Alvin was ranching country as well as oil country. When Ryan was twelve, he bought a two-day-old calf and fed it with a bottle. Later, he raised it in a rented pasture. He sold it when it was six months old, and used the money to buy more calves. Ryan never lost his love for ranching and cattle.

Of course, there was baseball. Ryan was six when he saw his first Major League Baseball game. But he hadn't seen it in person. He watched the "Game of the Week" on the family's first television set. The games came on each Saturday afternoon. For the rest of the week, radio had to do.

In 1962, Houston got its own major-league team, the Colt .45s. The team would be renamed the Astros in 1965 when the Astrodome opened. Before that the team played outdoors, but the fans didn't mind. They cheerfully sweated and swatted huge mosquitos. After all, they finally had major-league baseball!

Ryan was one of those enthusiastic fans. He listened to the Colt .45s and later the Astros, dreaming that one day maybe he'd be playing under that big dome, too.

He first played baseball by tagging along with big brother Robert and his friends. Ryan hoped to get into the game if the older boys were one player short. He and Robert also took turns pitching and catching in their back yard. If there were no baseballs to throw, Ryan would throw rocks, mostly at the turtles and snakes in a bayou near his house.

In 1956, when Ryan was nine, he began playing in the Alvin Little League. He was proud to make the team and receive his first uniform. The boys couldn't wear their uniforms to school, but they did wear their caps.

For years, a story went around that Ryan developed his strong pitching arm from helping his father deliver newspapers. But Nolan threw the newspapers with his left hand, although he pitched with his right.

Ryan played Little League ball until he was thirteen. He referred to himself "a good player, not a great player." But he did make the all-star team twice and pitched his first no-hitter. Nolan best remembers the day he first thought about playing in the major leagues. During an awards ceremony, he was standing with the other players, listening to a speech:

"One day," the speaker said, "one of you Little Leaguers will go on to play in the major leagues."

"It was like a bell went off in my head," Ryan wrote in *Throwing Heat*, his 1990 autobiography. "I became very excited. . . . The sun, standing in the field, the man's voice, his words. I never forgot it. It was a monumental thing in my mind."

Even so, basketball, rather than baseball, was Ryan's first love in high school. Alvin twice had season records of 27–4 with the 6-foot-2-inch Ryan playing center. Nolan even thought about playing college basketball.

Ryan had another love besides sports, and her name was Ruth Holdorff. She was two years younger than Nolan and first watched him play baseball when her older sister (who thought Ryan was cute) took her to Little League games. Nolan and Ruth had their first date when she was thirteen and he was fifteen.

His high school days were simple, easy, and lots of fun. He played basketball and baseball, going out with Ruth on Friday and Saturday nights and attending the First Methodist Church Sunday mornings.

In the mid-1960s, Nolan Ryan might not have been thinking too much about his future, but some other people were.

One of the Top Ten Arms

As a high school sophomore, Ryan began to show what would become his blazing fastball that would claim strikeout after strikeout. Lucky for Ryan, and for baseball, that this was the same time Red Murff entered his life.

Murff had been a scout for Houston, but in 1963 began working for the New York Mets. Only by luck did he first see Ryan in March 1963. Having an extra hour he stopped in Alvin to watch a high school tournament. Just about the time Murff took his seat, the Alvin coach changed pitchers. The new pitcher was Nolan Ryan.

The scout watched Ryan throw two fastballs. "You could hear that ball explode," he would say later. After the game he asked Ryan's coach, Jim Watson, if the pitcher he had seen was a senior. No, Watson told Murff, just a sophomore who was tall for his age. Watson, a former college football player, really didn't know much about coaching baseball. "We only played baseball," he said, "because the state made us."

Murff knew he had seen something special, and he didn't want the young pitcher messed up. Football coaches usually put athletes on weightlifting programs to give them more bulk. Murff feared Ryan might become muscle-bound; causing his arm muscles to lose their flexibility. He told Watson that Ryan had one of the ten best arms in the world and not to ruin it.

Watson was surprised to hear this. He knew Ryan could throw hard, but the trouble was, that was all he could do! His curveball and his control were terrible. No wonder opposing players were scared to hit against him. One player refused to bat if Ryan was pitching. A longtime Alvin resident said Ryan got many of his strikeouts because batters would swing at anything so they could sit down again.

Other scouts came to see Ryan, but only Murff showed real interest. The next year Murff sent the following report to the Mets: "Skinny, right-handed junior. Has the best arm I've seen in my life. Could be a real power pitcher someday."

Murff convinced the Mets' head scout, Bing Devine, to make a special trip to watch Ryan during his senior year. On the day Devine came, however, Ryan was in no shape to pitch. Watson did not know Devine was coming. Upset over two close losses, had given the team an extra-hard workout. He had Ryan pitch batting practice for thirty minutes.

Ryan pitched, or at least he tried to. He was wild, had no zip in his fastball, and he was hit hard by the other team. He left the mound in the third inning behind, 7-0.

Needless to say, Devine was not impressed. Ryan thought he had blown his one chance to pitch in the majors. Murff felt terrible, but he still believed in Ryan. The kid just had a bad day, he told Devine.

When the Mets drew up their list of high school players for the 1965 draft, Devine had Murff's reports on one hand and his own impression on the other. The club made Ryan a draft choice, but not a high one. He was taken in the eighth round and was the 295th player chosen.

Ryan was disappointed. If there were 294 players considered better prospects, it seemed unlikely he'd make it to the majors. The Mets offered him about $30,000 if he would sign a contract, but Ryan was undecided. Several scouts had recommended that he go to college and play baseball there. He thought that if he went to college, he might become a veterinarian someday. He also thought about quitting both baseball and school and getting a full-time job.

On June 28, 1965, Ryan, his mother and father, Murff, and a local sportswriter sat around the family's kitchen table. The contract lay in front of him and the pen was in his hand, but Ryan could not make up his mind. He wrote later that he finally decided after looking across the table at his father. Nolan thought about his dad's endless work. Morning after morning he delivered newspapers to bring up the six Ryan children. The eighteen year old signed the contract and became a professional baseball player.

Learning in the Minors

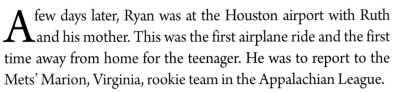

A few days later, Ryan was at the Houston airport with Ruth and his mother. This was the first airplane ride and the first time away from home for the teenager. He was to report to the Mets' Marion, Virginia, rookie team in the Appalachian League.

Ryan's doubts that he could make it as a pro soon grew stronger. There were more than forty ballplayers on the Marion team. Back home they had been stars. Here, everyone had outstanding talent. But some had more talent and determination. And these players were the ones who had a chance to make it.

Ryan's first manager was Pete Pavlick, who was almost a father to the players as well as a manager. He helped the youngsters adjust to new lives and new surroundings. But he also had some difficult duties.

Competition was keen, and only twenty players suited up for each game. The rest were left behind to practice. If you had too many bad days, Pavlick would call you aside and gently tell you that you had no future with the Mets. About seventy players were on the Marion team at one time or another that summer. Many were cut and went home, their dreams ended.

The Appalachian League was a long, long way from the glamour of the majors. Teams traveled in buses that frequently broke down. Playing fields were small, dark, and bumpy. Dressing rooms were crowded. The players were lucky if there were showers, and luckier if the showers had hot water.

Ryan pitched well, but not spectacularly. He had a 3–6 record and a so-so earned run average (ERA) of 4.38. (A pitcher's earned run average is the average number of earned runs given up for each nine innings pitched.) Ryan also had control problems, walking 56 batters and hitting eight in his 78 innings. What got the attention of the Mets, however, were his 115 strikeouts!

Ryan was one of only twenty Mets prospects invited to St. Petersburg, Florida, for the winter instructional league. Here, coaches worked with young players in a more relaxed atmosphere. Ryan worked with a pitching coach for the first time, and began to realize how much he had to learn.

He began the 1966 season with Greenville of the Western Carolina League in Class A. Baseball leagues are graded according to the level of competition. They range from the rookie leagues through Classes A, AA, and AAA to the majors.

In many respects, Ryan had a fabulous season. He led the

league in victories (17) and strikeouts (272). But he also led the league with 127 walks. He was so wild that he broke the arm of a fan carelessly leaning against the screen behind home plate.

It was in Greenville that Ryan's parents and Ruth watched him as a professional for the first time. He didn't disappoint them, beating Gastonia and striking out 19 batters.

When the Western Carolina League season ended, Ryan was assigned to Williamsport, Pennsylvania, a Class AA club. He was 0–2 there, but in one of those games recorded 21 strikeouts.

Ryan might have won his last game in Williamsport, but he

chose not to finish it even though he had a no-hitter going after four innings. He didn't have time to finish because he had to catch a plane for New York to join the Mets for the last few games of the season.

Only fourteen months had passed since that night in Alvin when he signed the contract. Now, he was headed to the Big Apple.

Nolan Ryan with his wife, Ruth.

World Series Success

As a new team in 1962, the Mets were supposed to be bad. And they were, winning only 40 games while losing 120. When their first manager, Casey Stengel, began working with the collection of rookies, misfits, and castoffs, he said in frustration, "Can't anybody play this here game?"

The Mets were better when Ryan arrived late in the 1966 season, but they still finished 30 games out of first place. They did not have anyone with a batting average .300 or better.

Ryan made his first major-league appearance on Sunday, September 11, 1966, against the Atlanta Braves. He entered the game in the sixth inning and promptly struck out Braves pitcher Pat Jarvis. Catcher Joe Torre got to Ryan for a home run in the seventh, but that was the only damage.

The New York Times recognized the importance of the event, even if it wasn't sure how to spell Ryan's name. The story the next day read: "For the Mets, the most noteworthy feature of an unproductive day was the debut of Nolen Ryan. . . ."

Maybe Mets manager Wes Westrum thought he was doing Ryan a favor by making the pitcher's next game a start against Houston in the Astrodome. Certainly Ryan was excited. He

This is the New York Mets 1969 team photo. Nolan is in the top row and is the fourth from the right (No. 30).

called his parents, and people in Alvin began making plans to be at the game on Sunday, September 18.

By the time some of them got to their seats, however, the nervous Ryan was out of the game, having lasted only one inning. He got three strikeouts, but he gave up four runs on four hits and two walks. And he hit a batter! Later, he wrote that no pitcher should make his first start in his hometown.

The 1966 season had been a good one. Between A, AA, and the pros he compiled 313 strikeouts and an ERA of 2.55. But Ryan knew he wasn't yet a big-league pitcher. He had simply overpowered hitters with his fastball. His short experience with the Mets showed him the need to develop a variety of pitches to succeed in the majors.

The Mets also knew Ryan wasn't ready. For 1967, the club assigned him to its AAA team in Jacksonville, Florida. If he did well there, he could be called up to New York. No one imagined that he would pitch only 11 innings all season.

First off, he got a late start. The previous fall he received a notice to report for a physical exam, the first step to being drafted into the U.S. Army. The United States was heavily involved in the Vietnam War. The Mets advised him to enlist in the Army Reserve. There he would spend only six months on active duty, rather than risk losing two years.

When his active duty ended, it was mid-summer. Ryan joined the Jacksonville team during a road trip and pitched three games in relief. During the last one, he continued to pitch even though his right forearm felt tight. Suddenly he felt a pop, almost like a rubber band snapping, and had to be taken out.

Ryan did not pitch again that season. He wasn't sure if he'd ever pitch again. But at least he had someone to help him through that difficult summer. He and Ruth had gotten married on June 26 in Alvin. People said it was like something out of a fairy tale. Ryan, voted 'Most Handsome' in his high school class, married Ruth, voted 'Most Beautiful' in hers.

That winter Ryan again went to the instructional league. His arm had healed and his fastball was back. He looked so good in spring training that the Mets made him part of their major-league pitching staff for the 1968 season.

His first start of the season, only the second of his career, also brought him his first major-league victory. It even came at the same ballpark as his first major-league loss, the Astrodome in Houston. This time it was a far more confident Ryan who took the mound.

The date was April 13, Easter Sunday, and Houston got plenty of eggs—goose eggs! Ryan struck out seven of the first ten batters he faced. He gave up only three hits and no runs before leaving the game in the seventh inning when a blister formed on the middle finger of his pitching hand.

He was bothered by blisters all season. In fact, he got a lot of publicity when he tried to toughen the fingers of his pitching hand by soaking them in pickle brine. Because of his injured hand and weekend duty with the Army Reserve, Ryan appeared in only 21 games all year and had a record of 6–9.

In addition, Nolan and Ruth did not like living in New York. It was especially tough on Ruth, who was alone when Nolan

Nolan Ryan and catcher Jerry Grote celebrate the Mets win that put them in the 1969 World Series.

was on the road. In Alvin they knew everyone. In New York people might not even know their neighbors.

Ryan was also worried about his father. Lynn Ryan, a heavy smoker, had been diagnosed with cancer that summer and had to have a lung removed. Nolan was glad when the season ended so he could get back to Alvin.

The 1969 season figured to be like all the others for the Mets, a mediocre team just hoping to reach respectability. But they surprised everyone, including themselves.

In mid-August, the Mets were nine-and-a-half games behind the Chicago Cubs and were given little chance to win their division. Then they caught fire and began gaining on the Cubs. They took a one-game lead on September 10 when Ryan beat the Montreal Expos on a three-hitter. On September 24, the Mets clinched the National League (NL) East title.

Ryan had appeared in only 21 games, pitching 89 innings and striking out 92 batters. He felt he hadn't made much of a contribution. But the NL Championship Series and World Series were different. Ryan entered the final game of the NLCS against Atlanta in the third inning. The Mets were behind, 2–0, with two Braves on base and nobody out. He worked out of that jam and wound up getting the win. This victory put the Mets in the World Series against the Baltimore Orioles.

The teams split the first two games of the World Series. In the third, Ryan snuffed out a Baltimore rally and earned a save. The Mets won the next two games and the series, 4–1. The victory was perhaps the biggest upset in World Series history. Ryan knew he had contributed to the team's success. But he still wasn't sure if his future was with the Mets, or even in baseball.

He had even more doubts after the 1970 season. He began well, but his Army Reserve duty caused him to miss many starts. Ryan was also deeply affected by the death of his father that summer. His record for the year was 7–11.

Ryan had a better start in 1971. By the end of June he was 8–4. But Ryan couldn't maintain his rhythm and finished the year 10–14. His 3.97 ERA was the highest he would ever have for a full season in the major leagues. He was unhappy with the Mets and with living in New York. Ryan asked general manager Bob Scheffing to be traded.

Players and coaches of the 1969 Mets got together in 2009 to celebrate the 40th anniversary of their championship. From left to right are Yogi Berra, Nolan Ryan, Jerry Grote, Tom Seaver, Jerry Koosman, and Duffy Dyer.

He and Ruth, pregnant with their first child, Reid, started driving back to Alvin the day the season ended. Ryan didn't want to stay even one more night in New York. In December he received a call from Scheffing. He and three other players had been traded to the California Angels for infielder Jim Fregosi.

Years later, the Mets realized the mistake the team had made. Whitey Herzog, then New York's director of player development, said "It might be the worst deal in history."

Record Breaker

Ryan's move to California was a much-needed change. He was across the country from the Mets, even in a different league. His military obligation was over and he could concentrate on improving his pitching. He felt that he needed this fresh start.

"I've been a disappointment to myself," he said. "If I didn't feel I had the potential to be a 20-game winner, I'd quit."

A few times that spring Ryan did want to quit. Pitching coach Tom Morgan and catcher Jeff Torborg worked with him to change his pitching motion. But whenever Ryan got into a groove, it never lasted long.

There were troubles off the field, too. A player strike meant

Ryan had no money coming in. He borrowed money from a bank in Alvin, and the family lived in a trailer home borrowed from Nolan's sister. He thought about quitting and heading back to Texas, but decided to stick with baseball a little while longer.

Despite a poor spring, he began the 1972 season in the Angels starting rotation. He won his first start, but by mid-May manager Del Rice wanted to put him in the bullpen. Morgan convinced Rice to stay with the twenty-five-year-old hurler.

Morgan spent hour after hour with Ryan. At last, something clicked. By midseason, Ryan had 10 victories. He made his first

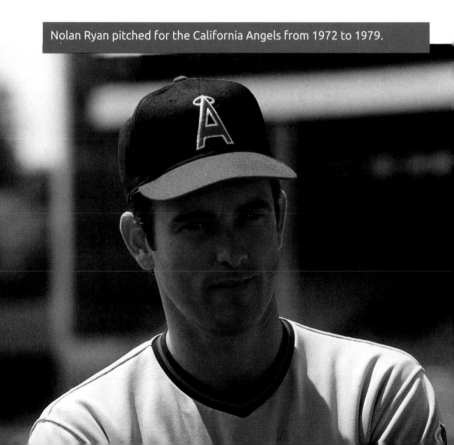

Nolan Ryan pitched for the California Angels from 1972 to 1979.

all-star team and almost became a 20-game winner, finishing 19–16. He led the league with 329 strikeouts and 9 shutouts.

Now Ryan felt he belonged in the majors. He and Ruth liked Southern California. He received a good salary increase and was looking forward to the next season. And what a season it would be!

The Nolan Ryan legend truly began on May 15, 1973. Until then, he was a promising young pitcher with a good fastball. Not many people knew about him, but that was to change. The 12,000 fans in Kansas City's Royals Stadium that night were the first to take notice.

Warming up, Ryan didn't feel all that confident. But through six innings the Royals hadn't gotten a hit. It appeared something special was happening.

Soon it was the bottom of the ninth. Royals shortstop Freddie Patek popped up to first. Then Steve Hovley struck out. That brought up Amos Otis, who had been a teammate of Ryan's with the Mets. After missing the first pitch, Otis hit the second offering deep to right. But it was not deep enough. Ken Berry ran back, made the catch, and Ryan had his first professional no-hitter!

"Ever since baseball people first saw Ryan's sizzling fastball, they said…there would come a time when they would send a ball to the Hall of Fame with his name on it," a reporter wrote.

It had just been a matter of time, his teammates said knowingly. But Ryan, modest as ever, claimed, "I never honestly felt I was the type of pitcher to pitch a no-hitter."

It was Kansas City's Patek who proved to be the best

prophet. "Is this his first one?" he asked after the game. "Well, I don't believe it'll be his last."

Patek spoke more truly than he knew. In exactly two months, Ryan became the fifth pitcher ever to throw two no-hitters in one season. The second one came against the Tigers in Detroit. Ryan knew warming up that it could be a big night. His fastball was moving and his curveball was hard and sharp.

He had almost no trouble through the first seven innings, striking out 16 batters. With one out in the ninth, Detroit's Gates Brown almost broke it up. But his line drive was straight at shortstop Rudy Meoli, who snagged it about a foot over his head.

The tension in Tiger Stadium was high, as it always is when a pitcher is one out away from a no-hitter. But the tension turned to laughter when the next batter, fun-loving Norm Cash, came to the plate carrying a table leg instead of a bat.

He claimed he had no chance with a bat against the pitches Ryan was throwing. But umpire Ron Luciano finally forced him to return to the dugout for a real bat. Cash was right the first time; he had no chance. On a 1–2 count, Cash popped up to Meoli in short left field.

Even though Ryan had thrown two no-hitters, his record was not spectacular. And he was his usual low-key self after the game. "I don't feel like I've done as much for the club as I could be doing," he said. "I hope things will be better now."

Things were better, indeed. He won eight of his last ten decisions. As the strikeouts kept coming, Ryan closed in on the single-season record of 382 by Sandy Koufax of the Los

Angeles Dodgers. He needed 16 more when he pitched his last scheduled game at home against the Minnesota Twins.

Ryan survived a rocky start. Minnesota scored three runs in the first. But he settled down and had 12 strikeouts through five innings. In the seventh inning he got 3 more strikeouts. One more for the record!

Ryan didn't strike anyone out in the eighth or ninth, but the game went into extra innings. He was exhausted and knew the tenth inning would be his last. First, he walked Rod Carew. Then, much to the crowd's disappointment, Steve Brye and Tony Oliva flied out. Ryan had one more chance.

The batter was Rich Reese. Ryan quickly blew two fastballs past him. After the second pitch, Carew tried to steal second. Without thinking that an out would cost Ryan a chance at the record, catcher Jeff Torborg threw to second to try to catch Carew. The Angels' fans cheered when the other team's runner was called safe.

Then, with the count 0–2, Ryan went into a stretch and fired a fastball with everything he had. Reese swung, missed, and Ryan had strikeout number 383!

Only one more thing was needed to make the 1973 season perfect, but it didn't happen. Although Ryan had a record of 21–16, Jim Palmer of Baltimore, with a 22–9 record, won the Cy Young Award. This yearly award is given to the pitcher voted best in each league.

Ryan was now a household name in Southern California. He was the prime attraction on a subpar team. In 1974 he had another very good year. Although his strikeouts were down to

Ryan acknowledges the crowd as they celebrate him breaking Sandy Koufax's single-season strikeout record. He whiffed Rich Reese of the Minnesota Twins to break the record.

367, he had one more victory, finishing 22–16. That last victory was special. It was his third no-hitter!

Ryan felt good before this September 28 game in Minnesota. He knew it would be his last start of the season, so he could hold nothing back. As he said to catcher Tom Egan, "What have I got to lose?"

Pitching coach Billy Muffett knew something was up. He told manager Dick Williams, "I don't like to say this, but warming up, he's throwing faster than I've ever seen."

He may have been faster, but not all that accurate. Ryan walked 8 batters. But he struck out 15, including Eric Soderholm for the last out. He was happy, but his mind was more on heading home to Texas with his family. It hadn't been a very good year for the team, which finished last in its division.

The 1975 season would not be good for the Angels or for Ryan. During April he developed a swollen and painful right elbow because of some loose bone chips. Still, he managed to win six of his first seven decisions.

The last thing he expected was a fourth no-hitter, but that's what he threw on June 1 against Baltimore. Three things made it one of the most important ones he has thrown: it tied him with Sandy Koufax for the most no-hitters, it was his 100th major-league victory, and most important to Ryan, it was the first time Ruth was there in person.

Baltimore's best chance for a hit came in the seventh. Angels rookie second baseman Jerry Remy fielded Tommy Davis's high chopper behind the mound. Remy snapped a throw to first, catching Davis by half a step. In the ninth, Ryan retired Al

Bumbry on a fly to left, got Davis to ground out to Remy again, and caught Bobby Grich looking at a changeup for strike three.

There was champagne in the locker room afterward, but Ryan turned it down. As he would do more than fifteen years later in Texas, he celebrated by taking Ruth to a quiet dinner.

Talk began that Ryan might become the second player ever to pitch two no-hitters in a row. The pitcher's next start was against Milwaukee, and he held the Brewers hitless for five innings. But Henry Aaron ended the streak with a hit in the sixth. Ryan went on to pitch a two-hit shutout, which is still a great game.

That game was the peak of the season. Ryan's elbow soon began to give him so much pain that even a simple thing like brushing his teeth was torture. He also suffered a badly pulled groin muscle.

Ryan's pitching began to go bad, and so did his attitude. He refused to talk with reporters, hiding after games. Finally, the pain became too much. He had elbow surgery in late August and his arm was in a cast until October. After having started out 10–3, he wound up with a record of 14–12 and fewer than 200 strikeouts.

Early in 1976, Ryan didn't know if he'd ever pitch again. He was now twenty-nine years old and his responsibilities had increased in January with the birth of his second son, Reese. He began to lightly throw a baseball again, just to see how the arm was. To his relief he felt no pain. He knew he would be able to continue.

The Angels continued to lose early in the season, but the

players' attitude and performance improved when pitching coach Norm Sherry replaced Dick Williams as manager. Ryan, 6–9 the first half of the season, won 11 games over the second half. He still finished 17–18, his first losing record in California.

Even so, he felt good. He had finished strong and his arm had completely recovered. He signed a three-year contract, and the Angels added some talented players. All this made him look forward to 1977. During spring training in March, Ryan had one more thing to feel positive about. That was the birth of his third child, daughter Wendy.

The 1977 season was, indeed, a good one for Ryan. But the Angels didn't do as well as expected. Nevertheless, Ryan had to be satisfied with his numbers. He won 19 games, led the league with 341 strikeouts, and posted an ERA of 2.77 (his best since 1972). In 1978 things were the other way around. The Angels won a team-record 87 games, finishing second. Ryan, though, was bothered by injuries. His 10 victories were his fewest since his last season with the Mets.

Ryan now felt comfortable in Southern California. He had one more year on his contract, and then could be a free agent. This meant he could sign with the team that would pay him the most. But he felt a special bond with the California fans and was happy with the Angels. That changed when he began contract talks with Buzzie Bavasi, who had been named general manager in 1977.

Ryan was making $300,000 a year. This was a lot, but far less than what some of the free-agent players were getting. Before the 1979 season, Ryan wrote Bavasi. He said he wanted

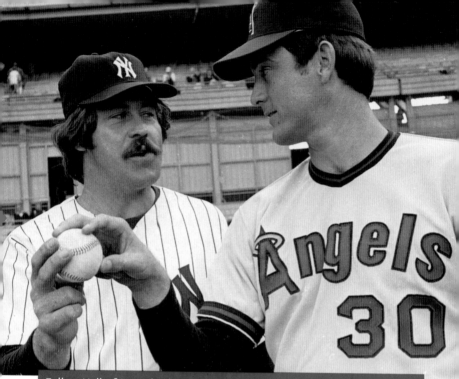

Fellow Hall-of-Fame hurlers Nolan Ryan and Jim "Catfish" Hunter talk pitching prior to a Yankees/Angels game in 1975.

to stay with the Angels and extend his contract for three years at $400,000 a year. Bavasi wrote back that they would discuss it after the season. When the season started, however, Bavasi began making unflattering remarks about Ryan to reporters. He declared him little more than just another .500 pitcher. Ryan made up his mind to file for free agency at the end of the year.

In 1979, Ryan struggled to a record of 16–14, though he still led the league in strikeouts, with 223. California, however, finally won its first division championship. The Angels playoff opponent was the Baltimore Orioles. Ryan started the opening game of the series and pitched seven innings, giving up only four hits. The Angels lost when pinch hitter John Lowenstein hit a home run in the tenth.

Ryan had made his last appearance in an Angels uniform. California lost the second game, won the third, but was eliminated in the fourth. So Ryan, who would have started the fifth game, never got another chance.

During the season, contract talks had become so bitter that Ryan knew he could never play for Bavasi. "If I had stayed with the Angels after the negotiations," he said later, "I don't know if I would have been able to push myself hard enough." When Ryan publicly said that he would not be back, Bavasi replied that replacing him wouldn't be that hard: "All I need to do is find two 7–6 pitchers."

When the free agent draft came, Ryan was picked by the New York Yankees, Houston Astros, Texas Rangers, and Milwaukee Brewers. He quickly got an offer of $1 million a year from Yankees owner George Steinbrenner. But Ryan and Ruth did not want to move back to New York.

There was only one place Ryan really wanted to play and that team matched the Yankees offer. Ryan was returning to Texas as a member of the Houston Astros.

Hometown Hero

Nolan Ryan was back in Alvin, but this time year-round. Ryan was far different from the rawboned kid who had left in 1965. He was thirty-three, an established star, and the first person ever to be paid $1 million a year by his team.

The money was something of a problem at first. Some people thought the Ryans would consider themselves above everyone else. Alvin residents soon found that Nolan was pretty much the same person who had delivered their morning papers. Ruth was not much different from when she was the high school tennis champion.

"We were more excited about the opportunity to play here than the contract itself," Ryan said of himself and his wife. Ruth added, "Now all our friends and family can suffer each game as I did for twelve years because he'll be right here."

Reporters in Houston wondered if anyone was worth $1 million a year, but the overall reaction was positive. "If there is any athlete in the world you would give a million dollars," wrote Mickey Herskowitz, "then Nolan Ryan is probably as good a choice as any…"

Millionaire or not, Ryan started slowly in 1980 and was bothered by back trouble. He eventually finished 11–10 and the Astros beat the Los Angeles Dodgers in a one-game playoff to win the NL West. His ERA of 3.35 was his lowest in three years, and for the first time in ten years he walked fewer than 100 batters.

Ryan started the second and fifth games of the NLCS against the Philadelphia Phillies. He pitched six and two-thirds innings the first game and seven innings the second. But the Astros lost both in the tenth inning. In fact, Houston lost three extra-inning games to the Phillies, who went on to win the World Series.

The 1981 season was a strange one for Ryan and for all of baseball. A strike by the players in mid-season lasted fifty-two days. Ryan spent it working on the cattle ranch he had bought a few years back. After the strike, teams that had been leading their divisions were the first-half champs. Those with the best records afterward won the second half. These teams would then have a best-of-five game playoff for the division championship.

The Dodgers had won the first half. And the Dodgers and Astros were neck-and-neck for the second-half title. On September 25, they met in Houston. Ryan started the second game of the series before a full Astrodome and a national television audience.

It had been six years since his last no-hitter. At age thirty-four, Ryan didn't know if he had another one in him. He breezed through the first six innings. But in the seventh, Dodgers catcher Mike Scioscia sent a fastball deep to right center. Terry Puhl sprinted toward the wall, got there in time, and made the catch.

That was as close as the Dodgers were going to get. In the ninth inning, Ryan struck out Reggie Smith on three pitches. Then he got Ken Landreaux to ground out, and retired Dusty Baker on a ground ball to third. The kid from just down the road in Alvin had broken Sandy Koufax's record of four no-hitters.

Houston won the second half of the season. Although they lost to the Dodgers in the playoffs, it was one of Ryan's best seasons. He was 11–5, the best winning percentage of his major-league career, and led the league with an ERA of 1.69.

Off the field, however, it wasn't that good a year. He had been a big loser in the baseball strike. Since

The Houston Astros signed Ryan to pitch for them prior to the 1980 season. Houston was very close to his hometown of Alvin, Texas, and the Ryan's were happy to go home.

the players weren't paid for games missed, he lost about $330,000.

Houston fell to fifth place in 1982, so the fans focused on whether or not Ryan would become baseball's all-time strikeout leader. He needed 259 to best the record of 3,508 by Walter Johnson. He fell 15 short, but still had a respectable year. He finished 16–12 while pitching 10 complete games.

In his first start of the 1983 season against the Montreal Expos, Ryan struck out seven. This included future Hall-of-Famer Andre Dawson for No. 3,500. He added three more against Philadelphia. His next start was on April 27 against the Expos in Montreal.

Ryan fanned two in the second inning, and one in the fourth. He tied Johnson's record by getting Tim Blackwell in the eighth. That brought up pinch-hitter Brad Mills. Mills took a fastball for strike one. He swung at another fastball, missing for strike two. Next, Mills took a third fastball for ball one. Clearly he was looking for another fastball. Instead Mills got a curve that broke over the outside corner. Mills stood completely fooled as the umpire signaled strike three!

Ryan finished the 1983 season 14–9. The 1984 and 1985 seasons were off years for the Astros and only so-so for Ryan. He was 12–11 in 1984 after going on the disabled list twice. In 1985 he was 10–12, recording his first year below .500 since 1978. One of the few highlights came on July 11, 1985, when he struck out Danny Heep of the Mets for strikeout number 4,000.

It looked as if 1986 would be much the same. But new manager Hal Lanier turned things around and the Astros won the NL West Division. Ryan compiled a record of 12–8 even though he was again on the disabled list twice with arm trouble. In his last ten starts, he was 5–1 with an ERA of 2.31.

The Astros won the first game of the NL Championship Series against the Mets. Ryan started the second game but was knocked out in the sixth inning as the Mets won 5-0. After the teams split Games 3 and 4, Ryan pitched the fifth game against Dwight Gooden in New York.

He pitched beautifully, yielding only one run on two hits in his nine innings. But the Mets won the game, 2-1 in the twelfth, and went on to win the series. The key play was a questionable call by umpire Fred Brocklander in the second inning that might have given Houston another run.

There was no trace of arm trouble when the 1987 season began. So Ryan was surprised when general manager Dick Wagner placed him on a strict limit of 115 pitches per game. Whenever Ryan reached that point, he would have to come out of the game. Ryan tried to convince Wagner that the limit was not needed. Wagner showed him statistics. He said that whenever Ryan threw more than 130 pitches a game, he pitched poorly in his next start.

The frustrated Ryan had the worst record of his career, 8–16. Yet his ERA of 2.76 and his strikeout total of 270 were the best in the league. Many times, he was forced out of the game by the pitch limit, perhaps with the team behind only 1-0, and wound up taking the loss.

He pitched so well that there was talk he might win the Cy Young Award. No pitcher had ever won the award with a losing record. Instead, the honor went to Steve Bedrosian of Philadelphia. It was the first time a pitcher ever led his league in both strikeouts and ERA and failed to win the Cy Young.

Ryan wrote in 1988 that he intended to spend the rest of his career with the Astros. But that season, an average one, turned out to be his last year with Houston. Ryan's record was 12–11 with a 3.52 ERA and a league-leading 228 strikeouts. He didn't get much help from his teammates. In Ryan's 11 losses, Houston only scored a total of 11 runs.

One good moment came on July 9, when he beat the New York Mets. The game was his 100th victory for the Astros. He was now the only player besides the legendary Cy Young to win 100 games for teams in both leagues.

But owner John McMullen had begun trying to save money

Waving his glove to the fans, Ryan celebrates his record-breaking fifth no-hitter. He achieved the feat on September 26, 1991.

on player salaries. When Ryan wanted a contract extension for the 1989 season, McMullen offered him $800,000—a 20 percent pay cut. He knew Ryan was eligible for free agency, but probably thought no one would want a high-priced player approaching his forty-second birthday. McMullen was wrong.

Ryan became a free agent and immediately received an offer from the Angels. California owner Gene Autry wanted him back. Ryan liked the idea of rejoining his old team, but other teams were also interested. San Francisco made an offer,

On July 11, 1985, Nolan Ryan struck out Danny Heep of the New York Mets for his 4,000th career strikeout. This is an image of Ryan pitching during the first inning of that game.

and Houston got into the bidding when McMullen realized his mistake. But it still appeared California was the favorite. Then a new team entered the race—the Texas Rangers.

Staying in Texas appealed to Ryan. Even though the Rangers' offer (said to be $1.6 million) was lower than California's, Ryan decided to stay close to home. He signed with the Rangers on December 7. Of the four offers, Houston's was the lowest, $1.3 million. If McMullen had made that kind of offer in October, Ryan might have stayed an Astro.

Ryan had wanted to end his career in Houston, but as usual, he was gracious. "I feel very fortunate to have had the opportunity to pitch at home for nine years," he said. "It's been very good for my family, and we're very appreciative of that. We appreciate John McMullen giving us the opportunity."

The Houston fans and media did not appreciate McMullen nearly as much. They were outraged that the Astros owner had let Ryan get away. "So Ryan is going to the Metroplex [the Dallas/Fort Worth area]," a *Houston Post* editorial ended. "Well, at least he'll remain a hero and a Texan, which is more than can be said for McMullen."

No one was angrier than the folks in Alvin. Mayor Allen Gray said he wouldn't go to a Houston game all year. People began making plans to fly to attend games in Arlington rather than driving to Houston.

The Houston Post writer Kenny Hand summed up how everyone felt about McMullen: "He has robbed us of our legend."

Hall of Fame Finish

Dallas-Fort Worth was just as happy as Houston was angry. The signing of Ryan was the latest of several moves by the Rangers, including trades for Rafael Palmeiro and Julio Franco.

"Nolan Ryan, in my opinion, is as fine a professional and human being as any organization could be associated with," said Texas manager Bobby Valentine, once a teammate of Ryan's in California.

General manager Tom Grieve called it "one of the greatest days in the history of this franchise." Ranger pitchers Bobby Witt and Jose Guzman were excited. Both had idolized Ryan growing up.

Ryan didn't disappoint in 1989, having what he called a "dream season." He had a record of 16–10, and his 301 strikeouts led the major leagues. It was the sixth time Ryan had struck out 300 or more in a season. At age forty-two, he was the oldest pitcher ever to do so. On June 14 he defeated his former team, the Angels, becoming the sixth player in history to beat every team in both leagues.

The most exciting moment of the season came late in August. Going into 1989, Ryan had 4,775 strikeouts. Most people thought he had a good chance of reaching 5,000 that year. As his strikeout total grew, the question was not whether he would reach it in 1989, but when?

When turned out to be August 22. He faced the Oakland Athletics needing six strikeouts to reach 5,000. It was a hot night in Arlington, but Ryan was just as hot. He struck out five batters in the first four innings. Then, in the fifth, up came Oakland's Rickey Henderson. It was just the second time he had ever faced Ryan.

Henderson worked the count to three balls and two strikes, the cheering growing louder with each pitch. With only one more strike needed, Henderson fouled off two pitches. Everyone in the stadium was standing. Finally, Ryan gunned a 96-mile-an-hour fastball low and away. Henderson missed it, and the 5,000th strikeout was in the books!

The game was stopped while Ryan waved his hat to the crowd. Baseball Commissioner Bart Giamatti was on hand. To Ryan's great surprise, even President George H.W. Bush offered his congratulations via a pre-recorded video shown on the huge center-field screen.

But Ryan had more surprises coming the next season. He

On August 22, 1989, Ryan reached the 5,000 strikeout milestone, and remains the only player ever to reach this number.

started strong, winning his first four starts. In May, he began to have back problems and was put on the disabled list. He rejoined the team June 6. His first start after coming back wasn't spectacular, but his second was.

The Rangers were in Oakland. Ruth and daughter Wendy were in the stands, while son Reese was in the dugout, rubbing his dad's back to keep it from getting stiff. Oakland's Walt Weiss got a walk in the third and Mike Gallego another one in the sixth, but that was all. Everyone realized another Ryan no-hitter might be on the way.

Rickey Henderson almost messed up the no-hit game. The speedy outfielder hit a slow roller. But Rangers shortstop Jeff Huson charged the ball, scooped it up barehanded, and quickly flipped to first. Henderson was out by a step. The game ended with Willie Randolph hitting a foul ball to Rubén Sierra in right.

This no-hitter was more satisfying to Ryan than any of the others. He had come very close to a no-hitter several times the previous year. But nine years had gone by since his fifth one. Also, at age forty-three, he was the oldest no-hit pitcher ever.

Another milestone was coming. Ryan had entered the season needing only 11 victories to become the twentieth player in history to win 300 games. He got number 298 in Detroit on July 14. A week later he got number 299 in Arlington.

Ryan failed on his first try for win 300, played July 25 in Arlington. He had better luck July 31 in Milwaukee. He pitched well, giving up three runs on six hits in seven and two-third innings. Relief pitcher Brad Arnsberg finished up to preserve the historic victory!

Ryan continued to have back problems throughout the 1990 season. Still, he managed a record of 13–9, leading his league in strikeouts with 232. It was his twenty-second season with 100 or more strikeouts, a major-league record.

In 1991, Ryan's right shoulder was giving him trouble. Ryan was 3–3, including that fabulous seventh no-hitter on May 1. But a strained shoulder muscle put him on the disabled list that month. After coming back he went 9–3 for the rest of the year. His 12 victories gave Ryan a career total of 314, three ahead of old Mets buddy Tom Seaver.

Ryan was in the last year of his contract. At age forty-four, he didn't want to change teams for a fourth time. And Texas was not about to risk losing its star attraction. In mid-season, Ryan signed a contract that would pay him about $3 million a year in 1992 and 1993.

The 1992 season was Ryan's most frustrating as a Ranger. He was bothered by several minor injuries. Relief pitchers often failed to hold a lead for him after he left a game. Some of his best efforts were wasted when the Rangers couldn't score enough runs. He failed to get a decision in any of his last four starts, even though he gave up only three earned runs in 27 innings. His five victories were the fewest on any of his full seasons in the majors.

It was no way to end a career, so Ryan didn't. On September 25, he announced plans to pitch again for the Rangers in 1993. "I certainly didn't cherish the thought of going out in my career with a season of this caliber," he said. "I think this ball club is in a position to be competitive, and I still think I can be competitive."

The 1993 season was Ryan's twenty-seventh, and last, in the majors. It is the most of any player in baseball history. He started 13 games that year and had a decent 5–5 record. Yet he recorded the worst ERA of his career (4.88) and only registered 46 strikeouts. The time had come to hang up the cleats.

In his first year of eligibility in 1999, Ryan became a Hall of Famer. He was formally inducted on July 25, 1999. He is only Rangers player to have his number (34) retired by the team. Ryan is also the only player ever to have his number retired by three different ball clubs (Angels No. 30, and Astros No. 34).

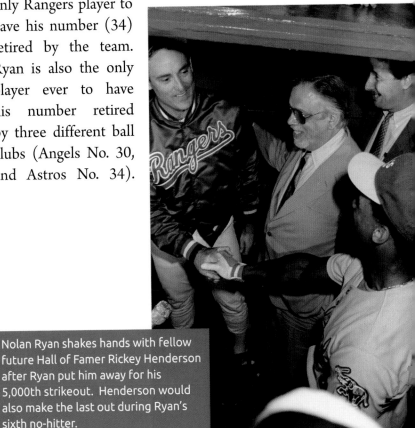

Nolan Ryan shakes hands with fellow future Hall of Famer Rickey Henderson after Ryan put him away for his 5,000th strikeout. Henderson would also make the last out during Ryan's sixth no-hitter.

In his enshrinement speech, he made it a point to thank the fans:

> *Last but not least are the fans. I feel very fortunate that I played with the four organizations that I did. I played on both coasts and I got the opportunity to stay in Texas for 14 years. And I can say that I was truly blessed by the fans and the support that they gave me and I do appreciate that. What makes this a great game is the support and the commitment that the fans give the game. And I may be gone, but I won't forget you. And I appreciate all those times that you supported me and my family over the 27 years that I played.*

Since his retirement from baseball, Ryan has stayed extremely active with new business ventures. He is a Principal Owner of the group Ryan-Sanders Baseball which owns two minor-league baseball teams: the Round Rock Express, which is a Texas Rangers affiliate team of the Pacific Coast League, and the Corpus Christi Hooks, a Houston Astros affiliate team of the Texas League. His two sons, Robert Reid and Nolan Reese, are both owners, and CEO and CFO of Ryan-Sanders Baseball. He has also owned banks and appeared in commercials.

Now that Ryan was retired, he also got back to his roots and opened up several cattle ranches down in South Texas. And since opening up these ranches, he started selling Nolan Ryan Tender Aged Beef, and eventually became a limited partner for the group that markets his beef, Beefmaster Cattlemen, LP.

On February 6, 2008 Ryan became the Texas Rangers' President. Before this, he had been with the franchise as a

During the offseason and after his playing career ended, Ryan invested in many ventures, including his own meat.

special assistant before leaving for the same position with the Houston Astros in 2004. Ryan eventually joined a group called Rangers Baseball Express. On August 12, 2010, the group finished their purchase of the Texas Rangers franchise, making Nolan part owner. But on March 11, 2011, he became the CEO of the Rangers. The Texas Rangers reached the World Series in both 2010 and 2011, becoming recognized as one of the most dangerous teams in baseball.

Standout

More than forty-five years has passed since Nolan Ryan threw his first major-league pitch. His former teammates were sometimes just as eager as fans to get his autograph. Former Texas third baseman Steve Buechele said, "There wasn't anything more exciting than coming to the games and watching Nolan pitch."

How did Ryan last so long? He claims that it was a combination of physical condition and mental attitude.

Ryan has always taken good care of his body. Even after the biggest of games, like his seventh no-hitter, he was up early, working out. "We're working against the clock," he told a reporter. "I can't do this forever. I haven't got much time."

He learned a balanced, healthy diet from his mother. She

Nolan Ryan and his wife, Ruth Ryan, take in a playoff game between the Texas Rangers and Tampa Bay Rays in 2010.

took pride in putting wholesome meals on the Ryan family table. Even as a young player he was careful about what he ate. He was even more careful toward the end of his career. He would avoid meats like bacon or sausage, cream soups, and any other food high in fat. He didn't eat fried foods and rarely ate large meals. When he snacked, he usually chose fruit.

Ryan's physical conditioning kept him going long after most players. He stayed fit during the winter. During the season, he maintained a workout schedule of weightlifting, throwing, and running that almost never changed. The times were very different from his early days in baseball, when all a pitcher did between starts was throw enough each day to stay loose.

Mental fitness probably had been just as important. Even

after his 27 major-league seasons, he still thought of baseball as fun and challenging. Yet, even though it was his living, baseball wasn't his whole life. He spent as much time at home with his family as he could. He was keenly interested in business and spent much time on charity work.

Off the field, Ryan was a family man and fan favorite. On the field, Ryan was a fierce competitor. White Sox third baseman Robin Ventura found this out the hard way when he charged the mound during a game in 1993. Despite being twenty years older, Ryan swiftly put Ventura in his place.

The talented pitcher never allowed fame and fortune to change his personality, as many star athletes have. Ryan remains what he always was, a modest, uncomplicated, man from a middle-class, family-centered background.

"I still represent small-town Texas, and that's fine with me," he once said. "I'm still like the people who lived where I grew up. I've kept my roots. I'm proud of that."

If you didn't know differently, you'd think Ryan was the man next door, working hard to put food on the table and tires on the car. "If you saw him in a shopping mall or talked to him in the grocery store, you'd think he was just another middle-aged guy," said a member of the Rangers organization.

Ryan wanted to be known and remembered as a "gamer," a player who went all out in every game. He was not afraid to pitch inside to a batter who tried to gain an advantage by standing closer to home plate. He'd make a batter duck or leap backward to teach him not to "crowd the plate."

With so many accomplishments so late in his career, Ryan was more famous as a Texas Ranger than he ever was as a Met, Angel, or Astro. There were crowds of fans and autograph seekers wherever the Rangers went. And Ryan's importance to the Rangers goes far beyond his pitching record. He was the player people came to see, and he now guides the organization.

Ryan still holds many major-league records, from the important (strikeouts, no-hitters) to the obscure (most assists by a pitcher in a five-game NL Championship Series). Some, like the ones for most walks and wild pitches in a career, he'd rather not have.

Ryan gives his Hall of Fame enshrinement speech in 1999.

Numbers, however, can't begin to explain the excitement Ryan brought to every game. You knew you would see history made with every strikeout. You could have been in on something truly spectacular, like a no-hitter.

In a country full of sports stars, he somehow stood out. Jim Murray of the *Los Angeles Times* wrote that even though we may have seen Mantle, Mays, Aaron, Rose, and all the rest, "I have a feeling when they talk of the second half of the 20th century in baseball, the most frequently heard question by our generation will be, 'Did you ever see Nolan Ryan pitch?'"

Career Statistics

Year	Team	W	L	G	IP	H	R	ER	BB	SO	ERA
1965	Marion*	3	6	13	78.0	61	47	38	56	115	4.38
1966	Greenville*	17	2	29	183.0	109	59	51	127	272	2.51
	Williamsport*	0	2	3	19.0	9	6	2	12	35	0.95
	New York	0	1	2	3.0	5	5	5	3	6	15.0
1967	Winter Haven*	0	0	1	4.0	1	1	1	2	5	2.25
	Jacksonville*	1	0	3	7.0	3	1	0	3	18	0.00
1968	New York	6	9	21	134.0	93	50	46	75	133	3.09
1969	New York	6	3	25	89.1	60	38	35	53	92	3.53
1970	New York	7	11	27	131.2	86	59	50	97	125	3.42
1971	New York	10	14	30	152.0	125	78	67	116	137	3.97
1972	California	19	16	39	284.0	166	80	72	157	329	2.28
1973	California	21	16	41	326.0	238	113	104	162	383	2.87
1974	California	22	16	42	332.2	221	127	107	202	367	2.89
1975	California	14	12	28	198.0	152	90	76	132	186	3.45
1976	California	17	18	39	284.1	193	117	106	183	327	3.36
1977	California	19	16	37	299.0	198	110	92	204	341	2.77
1978	California	10	13	31	234.2	183	106	97	148	260	3.72
1979	California	16	14	34	222.2	169	104	89	114	223	3.60
1980	Houston	11	10	35	233.2	205	100	87	98	200	3.35
1981	Houston	11	5	21	149.0	99	34	28	68	140	1.69
1982	Houston	16	12	35	250.1	196	100	88	109	245	3.16
1983	Houston	14	9	29	196.1	134	74	65	101	183	2.98
1984	Houston	12	11	30	183.2	143	78	62	69	197	3.04
1985	Houston	10	12	35	232.0	205	108	98	95	209	3.80
1986	Houston	12	8	30	178.0	119	72	66	82	194	3.34
1987	Houston	8	16	34	211.2	154	75	65	87	270	2.76
1988	Houston	12	11	33	220.0	186	98	86	87	228	3.52
1989	Texas	16	10	32	239.1	162	96	85	98	301	3.20
1990	Texas	13	9	30	204.0	137	86	78	74	232	3.44
1991	Texas	12	6	27	173.0	102	58	56	72	203	2.91
1992	Texas	5	9	27	157.1	138	75	65	69	157	3.72
1993	Texas	5	5	13	66.1	54	47	36	40	46	4.88
	MLB Total	324	292	807	5,386.0	3,923	2,178	1,911	2,795	5,714	3.19

*=Minor Leagues   IP=Innings Pitched   BB=Walks
W=Wins   H=Hits   SO=Strikeouts
L=Losses   R=Runs   ERA=Earned Run Average
G=Games   ER=Earned Runs

More Info

Where to write Nolan Ryan

Nolan Ryan
c/o Texas Rangers
1000 Ballpark Way
Arlington, TX 76011

On the Internet at:

http://www.baseball-reference.com/players/r/ryanno01.shtml

http://texas.rangers.mlb.com/

http://www.nolanryanfoundation.org/

Index

N

New York Mets, 15-29, 31, 37, 43-45, 52, 59
The New York Times, 23
New York Yankees, 39
no-hitter, 5-8, 14, 21, 31-32, 35-36, 42, 51-52, 56, 59-60

O

Oakland Athletics, 49-51
Otis, Amos, 31
Oliva, Tony, 33

P

Palmeiro, Rafael, 6, 48
Palmer, Jim, 33
Patek, Fred, 31-32
Pavlick, Pete, 19-20
Philadelphia Phillies, 41, 43, 45
Puhl, Terry, 42

R

Randolph, Willie, 51
Reese, Rich, 33
Refugio, Texas, 10
Remy, Jerry, 35-36
Rice, Del, 30
Round Rock Express, 54
Ryan, Lynn Nolan, Sr., 10, 26
Ryan, Reese, 36, 51, 54
Ryan, Reid, 28, 54
Ryan, Robert, 11-12
Ryan, Ruth Holdorff, 6, 9, 14, 19, 21, 25, 28, 31, 35-36, 39-40, 51
Ryan, Wendy, 37, 51
Ryan-Sanders Baseball, 54

S

San Francisco Giants, 46
Scheffing, Bob, 27-28
Scioscia, Mike, 42
Seaver, Tom, 52
Sherry, Norm, 37
Sierra, Rueben, 51
Smith, Reggie, 42
Soderholm, Eric, 35
St. Petersburg, Florida, 20
Stanley, Mike, 6-7
Steinbrenner, George, 39
Stengel, Casey, 22

T

Texas Rangers, 5-9, 39, 47-56, 59
Torborg, Jeff, 29, 33
Toronto Blue Jays, 5-6
Torre, Joe,

V

Valentine, Bobby, 48

W

Wagner, Dick, 44
Watson, Jim, 16
Weiss, Walt, 51
Western Carolina League, 20-21
Westrum, Wes, 23
White, Devon, 6
Williams, Dick, 35, 37
Williamsport, Pennsylvania, 21
Witt, Bobby, 48
World Series, 27, 41, 55